You have never met me...
I am the stranger everywhere...
sitting next to you on the subway...
selling newspapers on the street...
Begging for change on the corner...
Gazing out of a corporate building...
Playing in the park...
Driving your taxi...
Babysitting your kids...
creating the laws...
But always, always
Loving you unconditionally.
You don't need to know me
To know that you are loved.
So know that even in
All the pain you feel
You are never truly alone.
My prayers are with you
Your heart will heal
The sun will shine
And your loved ones
will reach
Their places with God.

Love always,
Kelly Nicole

page 1: Kelly Nicole, Chula Vista, California

opposite: Josh

Published and produced in 2002
by Welcome Books
Welcome Books is an imprint
of Welcome Enterprises, Inc.
Publisher: Lena Tabori
Project Manager: Natasha Tabori Fried
Editor and Art Director: Chris Jarrin
Designer: Jon Glick

Welcome Enterprises
6 West 18th Street
New York, NY 10011
Tel: 212-989-3200
Fax: 212-989-3205
www.welcomebooks.biz

Distributed to the trade in the U.S. and Canada
by Andrews McMeel Distribution Services
Orders Department and Customer Service
(800) 223-2336
Orders-Only Fax (800) 943-9831

Children's art and letters reproduced in this
book were so utilized in order to reach a
larger audience than had been originally
intended when they sent their letters to
Engine 24 Ladder 5. Proceeds from this book
will be donated to The Children's Aid Society
in order to help other children in need.

A special thanks to Ted Guidotti, Trish
Daley, Antonia Ludes and Leslie Lampe for all
your help.

Library of Congress Cataloging-in-Publication
Data on file.

Printed in Canada by Friesens Printers
through Four Colour Imports, Ltd.,
Louisville, Kentucky

First Edition
10 9 8 7 6 5 4 3 2 1

welcome
BOOKS
New York • San Francisco

do not be sad:

A Chronicle of Healing

Children's letters and artwork sent after 9/11 from across America to Engine 24 Ladder 5 FDNY

INTRODUCTION

CAPTAIN FRANK COUGHLIN, LADDER 5
CAPTAIN ANTHONY VARRIALE, ENGINE 24

IN THE DAYS, WEEKS AND MONTHS following September 11th, the letters contained in this book started piling up in our station house. They came in from every corner of the country from children we had never met.

During our very personal struggle with the loss of our brothers, the letters became a constant reminder that we were not alone. It was just amazing to think that in spite of all that was going on in these kids lives, they were taking time to let us know they were thinking of us.

The word hero comes up countless times in these letters. And to be honest, we don't know one guy in any company who sees himself as a hero. We see what we do as a job. A job we love. A job that most of us wouldn't trade for anything.

The support we have received has reinforced our belief in what we do. The letters we've gotten have given us tremendous strength and have broadened our sense of family. They are a tribute to our brothers, our city and our country. They have given us hope in a time of sadness. In many ways these have been the worst days and the proudest days of our lives.

top: Steven

above: Ladder 5, clockwise from left: Louie Arena; Eddie Foy; John Kelly; Mike Simon; Greg Wasserman; Frank Coughlin; Chris Cregin; Jerry Stepanyk; Paul Keating; John Santore; Jeff Anstead; Dave Clifford; Steve Napolitano; Frank McCutchen; Mike Brennan; Greg Saucedo; Tommy Hannifin; Darren Lebow

top: During the days that followed 9/11, children across the country sent messages of hope and encouragement

above: Katie, Harrison, Ohio

top: Charlotte, North Carolina

above: Lisa, Brunswick, Georgia

You don't need to
know me to know that
you are loved.

Kelly Nicole, Chula Vista, California

I am praying
for you. get better soon!

Love Liam

above: Liam

Dear firefighters of Ladder 5,

    I want to thank you for all your bravery, for going into the building to help others, and knowing maybe never agian you'll see your loved ones, your friends, or stepping outside agian for a fresh breathe.

    I understand only a little. I haven't lost someone like a mom, dad, a Grandma, or a Grandpa, but I've lost my pets, which isn't that bad, but still I was sad to lose them.

    That morning I remember waking up, seeing those towers fall, people crying hard, and seeing you guys trying to rescue people, I'm glad you never gave up, even when your friends have gone away.

Thank you
so much for helping
out!!!

From,
Bethany

above: Bethany, Portland, Oregon

I want to say
thank you, fireman
and policeman.

I love my uncle.
he was on
the plane.

top: Unsigned

above and opposite: Joey, Chula Vista, California

What happened to the twin towers?

above: Unsigned, Chula Vista, California

above: Cooper, Ft. Worth, Texas

16

clockwise from top left: Andy (Monroe Elementary); Unsigned, New York (NYC Lab School); Justin; Unsigned, New York (NYC Lab School)

above: Hafizul, Bronx, New York

I think the terrorists had bad parents.

Draven, South Lebanon, Ohio

opposite: Steven, South Lebanon, Ohio
overleaf: Unsigned, Chula Vista, California

Dear Firemen & women,
You weren't just there for the people that were trying to get out of the buildings.
You were there for little children that were confused about everything that was happening
and they just wanted there mom and dad to come home. Thanks for you mom and dad came
home. Thanks for you we only lost some but not all. I wish that I could of helped more, I wish
people weren't so mean but some people have a little more mean in them than they have nice.

Nicole, Reno, Nevada

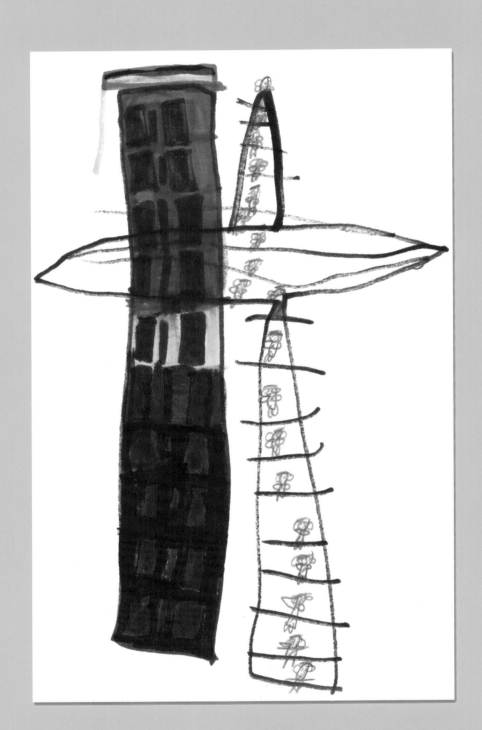

above: Torie, Ft. Mitchell, Kentucky

opposite: Troy, Shallotte, North Carolina

Twin Tawor

25

above: Jose, Clifton, New Jersey

opposite: Unsigned, Chula Vista, California

Dear God,
So many people are hurting [innocent] U.S. citizens. Please God can you tell me why they are doing this? I pray for the people that died in this tragedy and for the [families] that lost a loved one. Can you please help the people that are risking their life to find people [buried] in the soot and the rock. Please can you help them?

Andrew

26

above: Elisamuel

opposite: Blair, Wilmington, North Carolina

this page clockwise from top left: Unsigned; Katie, Willoughby, Ohio; Sean, Waymarnt, Pennsylvania; Michael, Wallowa, Oregon; Anthony, Finneytown (Brent Elementary), Ohio; Jonathan, Harwich, Massachusetts

this page clockwise from top left: Unsigned, Chula Vista, California; Kyra;
Unsigned, Massachusetts; Steven; Elizabeth and Sara, New York (NYC Lab School)

31

This is what I saw from the window!

I regret seeing it

above: Boris, Bronx, New York

opposite: Dylan, Ripley, West Virginia

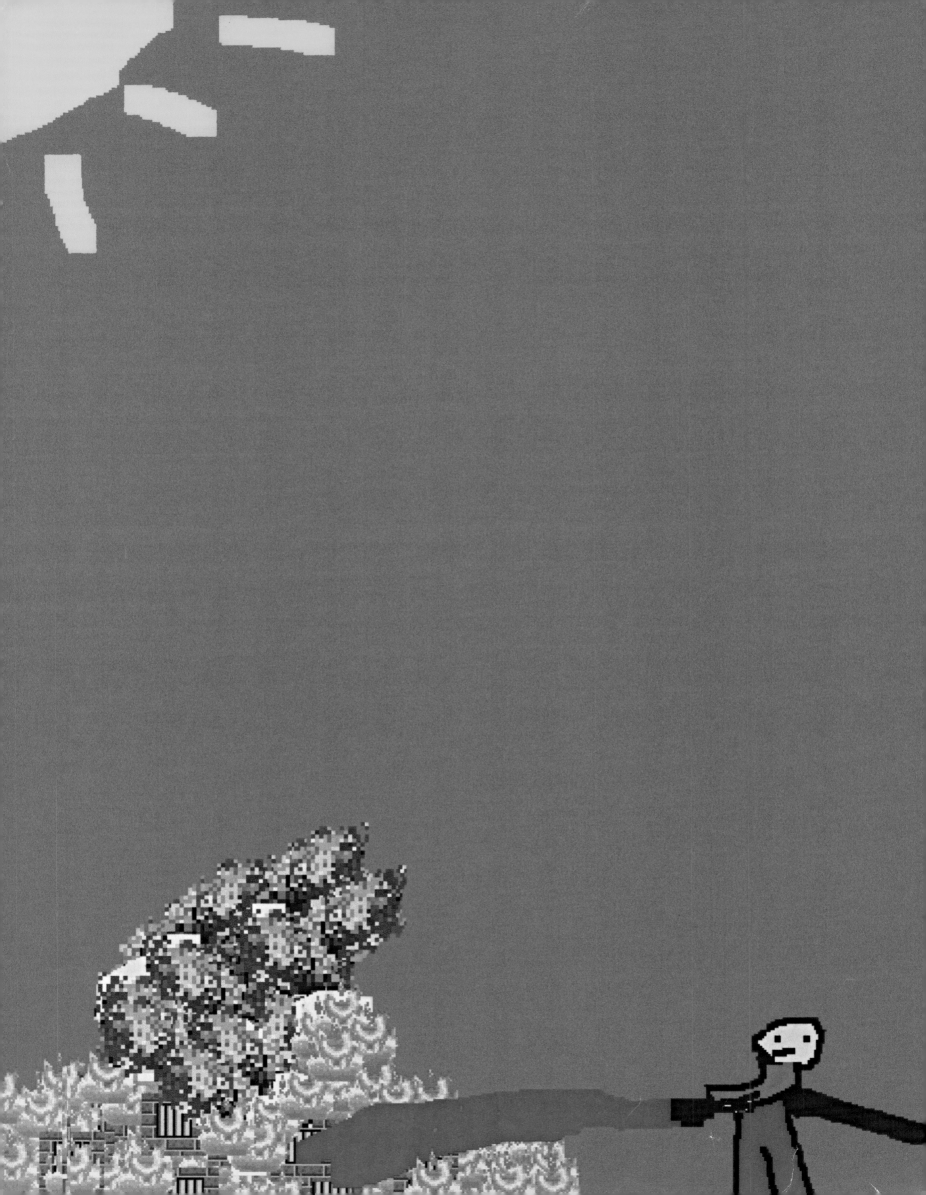

I know how hard it is.
Don't be sad.
You saved a lot of people.
You should be proud.

33

Tony (Edison Elementary School)

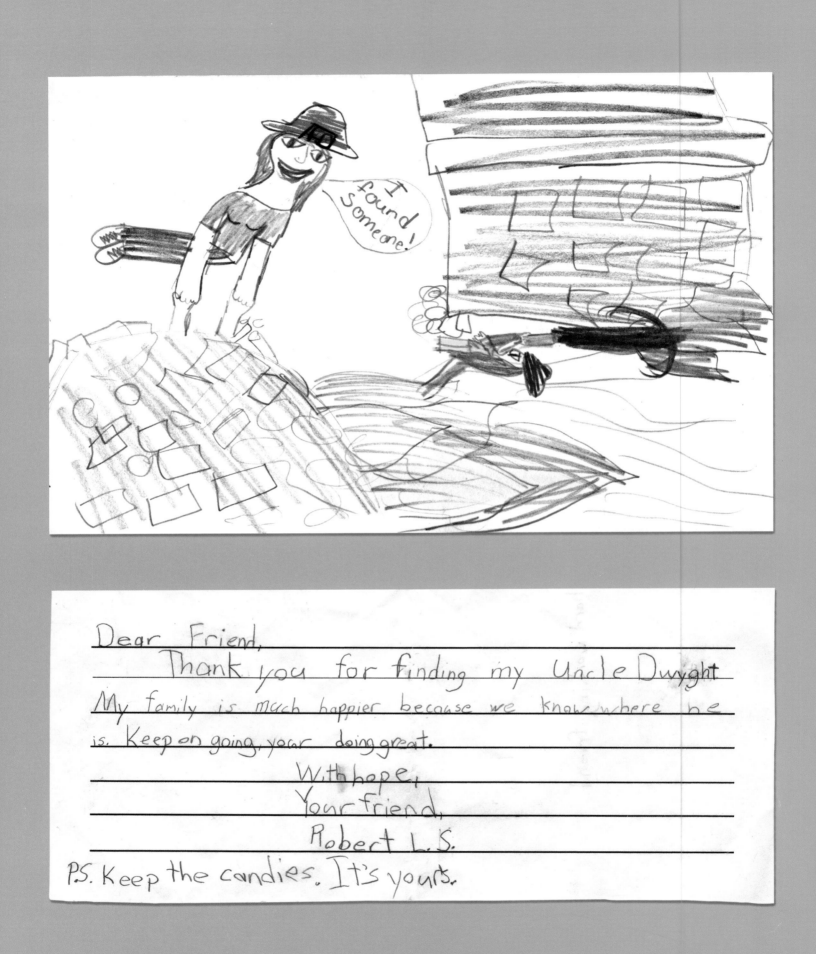

34

Dear Friend,
Thank you for finding my Uncle Dwyght
My family is much happier because we know where he
is. Keep on going, your doing great.
With hope,
Your friend,
Robert L.S.
P.S. Keep the candies. It's yours.

top: Rachel, New York, New York
above: Robert, Buckingham, Pennsylvania

Thank you very much for helping them. I very [much] appreciate what you guys did. You guys have influenced me in being positive in myself, and influenced me in being patriotic to my country. Because I know that I love my country and I will stand by it no matter what happens.

We are all united and no explosions are going to [separate] us. We will be united as nation and we are going to pass this tragedy. Thank you so much for helping us and my blessings go to you guys. I feel so happy that we have people like you guys who help us when we are in need. We cannot lose hope nor faith in our country, cause I know we will succeed. I really know it!

Jonathan, Chula Vista, California

35

above: Dylan, Newport Beach, California

God Bless
N.Y.

We will not be beaten

God bless Amarica!

above: Unsigned

opposite: Nick, Johnston, Rhode Island

Dear Fire Fighters,
You Make ourworld
Wonderful!   Love Jenne

you all can bet anything
in the world.

top: Jenny, Toronto, Canada

above: Unsigned, Chicago, Illinois

opposite: Sara, Burlington, Kentucky

38

N.Y.F.D. Engine 4

Dear Super Heros,

Thank you for saving
the in the, bulbding. I'm sorry
you lost your friends, I think
I know how you feel because
my Grandpa died. You are all
in my prayers.

Your Friend,
Sara

Good Job
Sparkey

this page clockwise from top: Jim, Green Forest, Alaska; Brett, Laguna Beach, California; Vladimir, Phillipsburg, New Jersey; Jazmine; Chris, Massachusetts; Sean, Hillsboro, Ohio; Joshua, Pauls Valley; Carlisle; Andrew, Portland, Maine

God bless America

The Firefighters

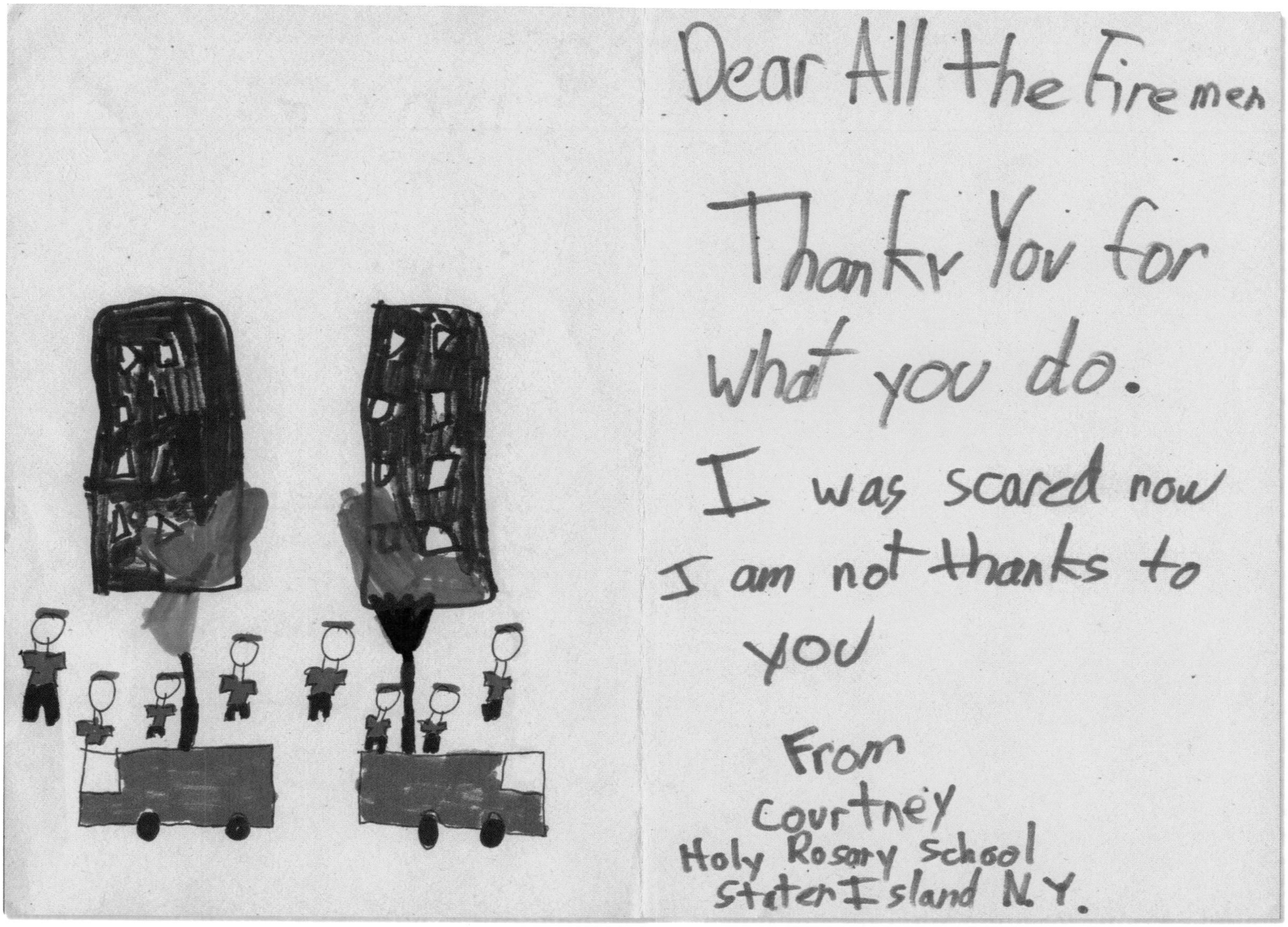

Dear All the Firemen

Thank You for what you do.
I was scared now
I am not thanks to
you

From
Courtney
Holy Rosary School
Staten Island N.Y.

above: Courtney, Staten Island, New York (Holy Rosary School)

opposite: Unsigned

Dear firemen,
Who have gave their lifes up for others who they
could save. While the enormus burning Flames were
crakling and when the building was starting to colapse
Some survived and many did not. For those who have
survived are to be greatfully honored. To me it might
be exhausting running back and forth saving people.
Sincerly,

Ashley Rae

above: Ashley Rae

44

To me it might be exhausting running back and forth saving people.

Ashley Rae

Though I don't know anyone in New York, it seems that a part of my own family has perished. My family of this proud nation. I just want to thank you and encourage you not to lose hope, because I'm not giving up on you or your friends. It's people like you that make me strive to become a hero and help the way you are right now. I'm so happy I can write to you, because while your not Zorro, Superman, or Batman, you are *my* hero in that you are helping save lives. I only hope that when I grow old enough I can be as honorable as you are.

Heather, Chula Vista, California

A hero is a person of great strength and courage. You are an example of a hero to me. With your help America will get back on its feet much quicker. It is an honor to all Americans to have so many dedicated volunteers. from someone who cares,

Stephanie, Quakerton, Pennsylvania

46

above, left to right: Joe, Kittery, Maine; Sarah, Johnston, Rhode Island; Chad, Laguna Beach, California; Kaylem, Chula Vista, California

opposite: Brooke, Hammonton, New Jersey

above: Katherine

top left: Hailey, Rockwall, Texas; top right: Roger, Phillipsburg, New Jersey

above: Joseph (Shell Point Elementary)

this page clockwise from top left: Eddie, Hammonton, New Jersey; Morgan; Jake, Reno, Nevada;
Ross, Mandeville, Louisiana; Abbey, Topton, California; Brad; Courtney

this page clockwise from top left: Adam, Whitehall, Pennsylvania; Third grader, Chicago, Illinois; Elise; Sifath, Bronx, New York; Elizabeth, Cincinnati, Ohio; Unsigned; Meredith, Hillsboro, Ohio

New York is still
Standing!
And So are
You!

Let freedum rring

above: Alex, Cincinnati, Ohio

opposite, clockwise from top left: Alex, Mason, Ohio; Juaneisha, Cincinnati, Ohio;

Aaron; Katrina; Cara, Cincinnati, Ohio; Katie, Burlington, Kentucky

Who would have ever thought that you would be given the ultimate challenge? Who would've ever thought that you would become our national heroes? Just last Monday, everything was fine and then tragedy struck. Each of you began a journey that would change your lives, as well, as the nations lives forever. Your journey will not go unnoticed. New York City's the greatest city in the world. New York City has the strongest foundation in the world. Your lives, and the lives that we've lost will become part of the city and its foundation. Stay strong and God Bless You.

Liecia, New York, New York

above: Timmy, Birmingham, Michigan

opposite: Dylan, Birmingham, Michigan

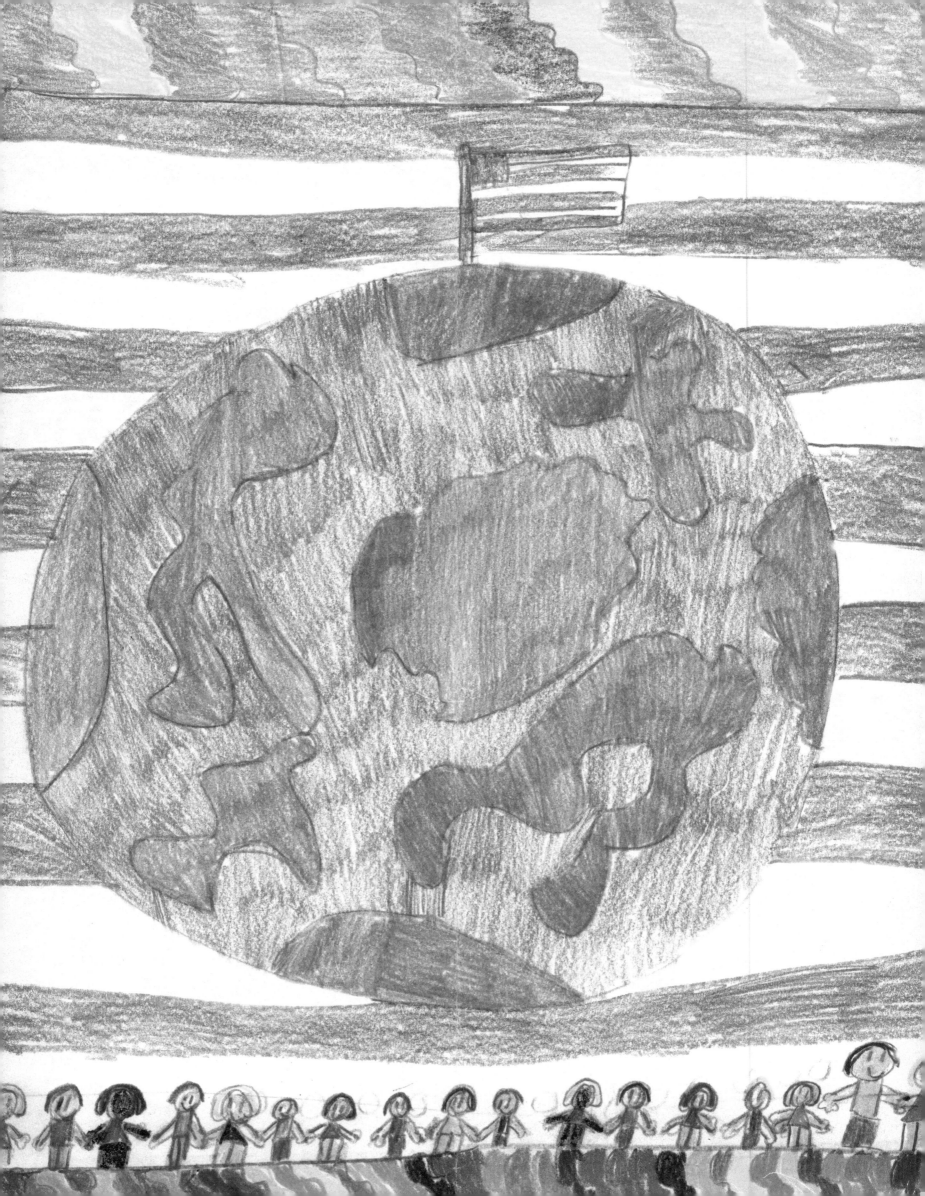

I want to be a rescue
worker. I'd like to work
like you but I'm just 8.

Leanna, Riverton, Illinois

opposite: Ashley, Waymarnt, Pennsylvania

To Our Heroes,

All of us here at Pine Bush High School want to thank everyone

working so hard; all the rescuers, volunteers, and medical personell.

Our prayers go out to those trapped and to the families that have

loved ones who are working or who have been a victim. Keep up the

good work.

Thank you
mike

Thank you Miki

Thankyou for all your hard work your our heros God bless you. Love brother

Love and support Evan

Jennifer

Joe

Thank you so much! Your in my prayers Lindsay

You're in our thoughts and prayers.

Thanks so much Rebecca

Thank you majid

Extreme thanks,

Ryan

Thank you For your Hard work L.J

Thank you so much for helping our nation in this horrible tragedy

America's heroes

doing a good job. Sincerely Jessica

Thank you for what your doing Dustin

Thankyou. thoughts and prayers all those effected. together we will get through this tradegy Matt

Thank you Evan

days

Thank you so much. It is greatly appreciated. You guys are great! Jessica

Thank You Lindsey

Colleen

Nick
Thankyou to all who help this tradjedy Jon

Thankyou god bless you, we here.

Hang in there thanks Jon Singer bless

Thanks so much— take care

Thankyou god bless you. dont give up.

A.J. DeWitt

Shane W. Stephanie

Stephanie Dw

Thanks alot you all did a good job

Bryan

Heather

Thank you for their help time of tragedy L.

Thank You

Thank you Michael

Thanks so much, your really making a difference -Kelley

Darly

Thanks Jon

Thank you and God bless!

hand prints from Kaukauna, Wisconsin, left to right: Darian; Gina; Kenlan; Nicholas; Jonathan; Emily; Ryan; Rose

I appreciate every action and every step your taking to help families and survivors. Because of you, your making the world a better place.
Keira

Find some People 64

My Deepest Gratitude. Thank you so much. Rachel

Keep up the good work!!! Tim

Thank you so much! I appreciate what you are doing and I hope everyone is okay
Katrina

You've earned the respect of us all Bill

Good Job Brian

Thank you For all You've done God bless America! ♡-Aimee

Thanks for everything

Apprieciate everything

doing to help. GOD BLESS

MUCH LOVE, AND

Thank you for everything... God bless.

God bless ♡ Juliane

you all are modern day Heroes! Christina

You all are modern day Heroes!

Thanks for your help in this time of tragety. We all appreciate your work. God bless. ♡ Sally

thanks for everything you guys/girls truly are heros Jessica

My prayers are with you. Amanda

God bless everyone with families with Lexington+006+ heros that work. Oh. god bless! Jess

Thank you! God Bless

Thanks for all you are doing to clean up.

Thanks for everything that you are doing. You make us proud! -Krystal

signatures, opposite and above: Pine Bush High School

Thanks For cleaningup.

top: Cody

above: Joshua, West Simsbury, Connecticut

above: 6th grader, Georgia

this page clockwise from top left: Cassie; Ethan; Unsigned; Sidra, Chula Vista, California; Unsigned, Brunswick, Georgia; Gus

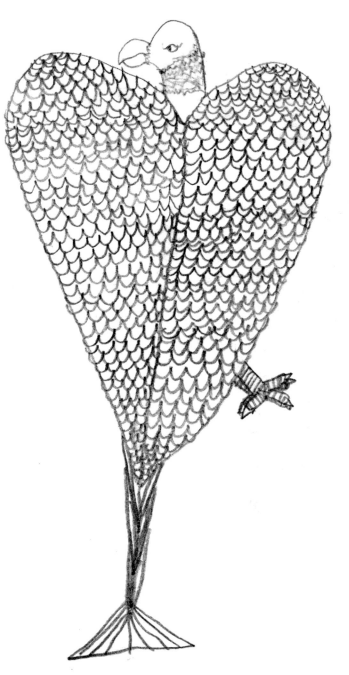

this page clockwise from top left: Katie; Mychal, Joy, and group; Unsigned; Josh, Rohnert Park, California; Catherine, Clifton, New Jersey

Dear Ladder 5,
America thanks you for your bravery
and courage. For going in to The World Trade
Center. When the planes flew into them. For
saving peoples lives and knowing you might
lose yours. For helping people by giving
blood, I thank you america thanks you for
everthing

Sincerly
Ryan

64

above: Ryan, Portland, Oregon